# Prague -
# *Lesser Town*

*Text* Mojmír Horyna
*Photography* Jan Reich

*petit*

# Prague - *Lesser Town*

## THE TOWN BELOW THE CASTLE

Mojmír Horyna, Jan Reich

PRAGUE — *MALÁ STRANA*

Translated by Derek Paton
Graphic layout by Aleš Krejča
First edition 1993
Petit Publishers Ltd, Dražického nám. 10, Praha 1-Malá Strana
Printed by Svoboda Ltd, Sazečská 8, Praha 10-Malešice

ISBN 80-901239-1-0

*...there lives in Prague a powerful and domineering guardian spirit, whom no one can escape when contemplating things of culture and art from above the Vltava River. That spirit has become the vital force which has come to rule the city with an iron hand: its powerful and famous voice rings out, sings, and sobs in the evening harmonies of Prague bells; its passion comes thundering towards us from the roar of the Vltava's weirs; its green domes, dedicated to eternal spring, have melded with Prague's wooded hills and heights in a natural unbreakable unity — only after the violent emotions and lofty thoughts of that divinity had been projected into the buildings and statutes was the artistic reality of Prague complete.*

*Arne Novák,*
*a leading Czech literary critic and historian*
*(1880—1939)*

When looking across the Vltava from the embankment in the Old Town or from the area around Charles Bridge, a breathtaking panorama appears before our eyes. The soft line of the ridge of Petřín, Strahov and Hradčany encloses a wide basin, providing room for a picturesque grouping of the towers, roofs and domes of one of Prague's most historical parts — Malá Strana (the Lesser Town). Its composition is remarkably strong, and together with the axis of Charles Bridge it creates a scenic effect. The arrangement of forms on the steep slope west of Hradčany, in particular, recalls the rhythm of views in a Baroque theatre. With the monumental appearance of Prague Castle which rises above the horizon like a painting on a wall, it is countered by the cupola and belfry of St Nicholas's Church. The effectiveness with which it links the Castle and city provides evidence of the incomparable mastery of its creator, a native of the town, the architect Kilian Ignaz Dientzenhofer, who was one of the greatest artists of the European Baroque.

It is no accident that a first look at Malá Strana should remind one of Baroque paintings and scenes. Baroque is the period which shaped this part of town definitively and imprinted it with uniqueness. The relationship of the composition of Malá Strana to the landmarks of Prague Castle and Strahov monastery is also no coincidence, because Malá Strana was linked by fate with the royal throne and the institutions of the Church. The former allowed Malá Strana to be founded, the latter gave it the majority of its artistic content. These two powers were uniquely linked and though at times in conflict the link was intensified in the eventful history of the town called Malá Strana.

# A CONCISE HISTORY & THE ARCHITECTURAL DEVELOPMENT OF MALÁ STRANA

*THE BEGINNINGS OF SETTLEMENT IN MALÁ STRANA*

The territory of present day Prague, situated on both banks of the Vltava river, which makes an extensive meander here, has been the site of human settlement since ancient times. The larger and longer lasting of the ancient settlements preferred a higher position which was further downstream on the northern and northwestern edge of today's city. The same is true of the early historic settlement (until about AD 700). On the territory of what is today Malá Strana were only smaller settlements where Mostecká ulice (Bridge Street) and the upper (western) side of Malostranské náměstí (Lesser Town Square) are now located.

The birth and development of a settlement on this site received their impetus from the fundamental event of early Czech history, namely the moving of the royal residence of the Przemyslides to the eastern and steepest part of Hradčany ridge, close to the crossing of important long-distance roads over the Vltava. (There used to be a ford north of where the Charles Bridge is today, which led to the area of Klárov, on the left bank. This occurred in about the middle of the ninth century when Christianity was first entering Bohemia and the medieval Czech state was just getting established.

## PRE-ROMANESQUE AND ROMANESQUE SETTLEMENT BENEATH THE CASTLE

To the south, under the newly established prince's Castle, the structures of the settlement were formed by the tenth and eleventh centuries. Its core was the area below the Castle, the central marketplace, and especially the rows of houses. Important roads from the ford on the Vltava to the Castle and further west went through here; they determined the basic lines of today's Malá Strana (the lines of Letenská street, the dead-end street Zlatá Studně, and Valdštejnská, Sněmovní, and Karmelitská streets are all of early medieval origin).

The fact that four churches stood here — St Václav (Wenceslas), St Martin, St Michal and St Ondřej (Andrew) — also testifies to the importance and density of the population of the area beneath the Castle in the eleventh century. All of the churches were located below what are today the squares Pětikostelní and Horní Malostranské, which formed the core of Malá Strana.

In the vicinity of the settlement below the Castle there were several smaller, rural settlements whose churches appeared predominantly in the twelfth century. In the area of what today is Klárov, near the ford over the Vltava, was the Rybáře (i.e., fisherman's) settlement with the

Church of St Peter, the patron saint of fishermen — who were the main residents of the area. Above the street now called Vlašská was the Obora settlement with the Church of St Jan Křtitel (John the Baptist), after whom the area Jánský vršek (St John's Heights) is named. The present network of streets is based on the urban plan of the early medieval village. The village of Trávník, with the Church of St Procopius, spread out around the village green at what today is the square Maltézské náměstí. The ancient Roman building materials remain concealed in the walls of the private dwelling on the southern part of Prokopská street, which has undergone radical Baroque and Classical reconstruction. To the southwest of Trávník was the smaller village of Nebovidy; its Romanesque Church of St Vavřinec (St Lawrence) still stands, after a couple of reconstructions, in Hellichova ulice. There were other villages to the south: Újezd, with the Church of St Jan Křtitel Na prádle (St John at the Wash-place) and the Church of St Jan Evangelista, which has long since disappeared.

[7]

The turning point in the development of Romanesque Prague was the period during the rule of the prince and later king, Vladislav II (1140—1173). During this time, significant buildings of monumental character came into existence in Malá Strana and its neighbourhood,

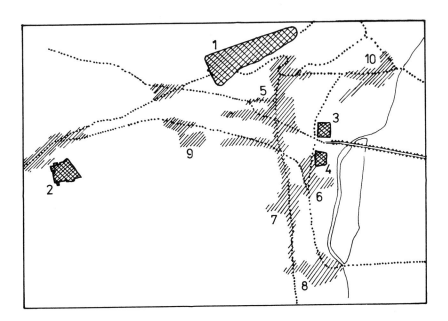

*The extent of settlements, main routes, and fords over the Vltava in Malá Strana in the Early Middle Ages*
(1— Prague Castle, 2— Strahov Monastery, 3— Bishop's Court, 4— Headquarters of the Knights of St John, 5— Area below the Castle, 6— Trávník Settlement, 7— Nebovidy Settlement, 8— Újezd Settlement, 9— Obora Settlement, 10— Rybáře Settlement (also known as Na písku)

which substantially influenced the shape of the settlement. The stone Judith Bridge, built about 1158 to replace an older, wooden bridge (mentioned by the chronicler Kosmas), had the greatest impact.

The main link between the two banks of the Vltava now shifted definitively to the south to approximately where the Charles Bridge now stands. The change in the ford's location brought about certain changes in the network of streets. It was at this time that Mostecká street, still the main artery of lower Malá Strana today, came into being.

The *Judith Bridge* represented a demanding construction of remarkable quality. It was located a bit further south of where the Charles Bridge is now and ran almost parallel to it. It made a striking turn to the south before the embankment at Malá Strana. The mighty stone tower of the Romanesque bridge remains preserved in the southern, lower tower at the Malá Strana end of the Charles Bridge. An excellent example of the artistic level of construction is the monumental Romanesque bas-relief on its eastern facade which is among the most important sculptural works of art of the twelfth century.

Probably beginning in 1158, the *hospital and headquarters of the order of the Knights of St John of Jerusalem* were built; Prince Vladislav met John of Jerusalem while on a crusade in 1147. The area around what is today Saská street and the eastern part of Maltézské square belonged to this order. The headquarters of the Knights of St John plus the Church Panny Marie Pod řetězem (Our Lady under the Chain) formed the core of a fortified enclave. The masonry of the headquarters can be found in all three wings of the high priory rebuilt in the High Baroque. The originally Romanesque church was a three-naved basilica with a transept and three apses, but only small fragments remain. In the twelfth century there already existed cross vaulting in the church and the ground floor of the headquarters.

Opposite the area of the Knights of St John, north of the Judith Bridge, another monumental and probably fortified complex of buildings, the *Court of the Bishops of Prague*, came into being at the end of the twelfth century. It was located at what was later the convent of the Carmelites; today it is the area taken up by the Ministry of Finance and Dražické square.

Beyond the area of Malá Strana, but still on its western horizon, the magnificent building of the first Premonstratensian monastery in Bohemia was built, in 1142, at the edge of a forest, (which had earlier been the deserted Strahov hill) after the foundation of a monastery named Monte Sion. Its monumental quality and its artistic expression is unparalleled in Bohemian Romanesque architecture; and it had a profound effect on building activity in Prague.

Fragments of the secular stone buildings from the end of the twelfth and beginning of the thirteenth century are preserved to this day. One of the most important structures was the spacious Romanesque courtyard on the spot where building No. 376 now stands at the corner of Prokopská and Karmelitská streets; its large cellars still remain. Similarly, buildings south of the Church of Our Lady under the Chain contain Romanesque stone work in their cellars. Also of Romanesque origin are the small fragments in the houses on the west side of Karmelitská street, where in No. 387 one finds remnants of the Romanesque Church of St Mary Magdalene.

## THE GOTHIC CITY, ITS FOUNDING, BLOSSOMING, AND DEMISE

The rule of Ottakar II (1253—1278) brought about the watershed in the history of Malá Strana. In 1257, the settlement below the Castle was promoted to the status of town. This change was accompanied by the dramatic demolition of the old settlement, the expulsion of its residents, the surveying of new foundations for buildings and the settling of a new population. The reasons for this change were mainly political and defensive. Evidence of this is the linking together of the city's fortifications, the royal Castle, the headquarters of the Knights of St John and the Bishop's Court at the Judith Bridge. The settlement on the west bank of the Vltava was thereby transformed into one fortified complex, which confirms the military aims behind the founding of the city as part of bolstering the defence of Prague Castle and controlling river-crossings via the Judith Bridge. The Malá Strana gate was incorporated directly into the fortifications and was given additional support by the proximity of the strongly fortified area of the Knights of St John and the Bishop's Court.

A city was gradually built in this newly demarcated area, beginning in 1257, along new and extremely regular lines. Its core was the spacious rectangular areas of what is upper and lower Malostranské square. Following the Przemyslides' thirteenth-century urban planning, which was based on plans from Classical Antiquity, the streets to the square led exclusively into the corners and centers of the sides. From there, the lines of today's Nerudova and Zámecká street, the southern part of Sněmovní and Tomášská streets, the western part of Letenská street, as well as the northern part of what today is Karmelitská street. The irregular diagonal location of Mostecká street was determined by the Judith Bridge. Some other little medieval streets had, of course, already disappeared (for example, a little street running alongside the Castle, which had been very important from the point of view of defence, can only be seen now as the outlines of upper Malostranské square at its southwest corner).

The remnants of the early medieval layout were preserved only in the northern parts of Malá Strana in what today is Pětikostelní plácek (Little Square of Five Churches). A new urban design was implemented using strikingly regular houses which ran through the whole depth of the block; the actual houses stood in the front part of the lots and the back tracts were predominantly wooden and had small gardens. In the second half of the thirteenth century other landmarks appeared. The parish church of St Nicholas (1293) stood on the square but then disappeared completely during the Baroque building of the Jesuit church and seminary. On the northern side among these buildings stood the older Romanesque church of St Wenceslas, as well as other parish houses, a school, the first town hall and some butcher shops.

On the eastern part, an exceptionally important building project began in 1285: the *cloister of the Augustinian Hermits* with the Church of St Thomas, founded by King Wenceslas II. The presbytery of the monumental three-naved church was consecrated in 1315; the triple nave was completed in the middle of the fourteenth century. The creative atmosphere of the original buildings of the monastery and the church was exceptionally mature. With these buildings the trend of post-classical Gothic came into being in the Malá Strana area; it was an extremely expressive form of architecture that tended towards a spiritual, ethereal style. The masonry of this period still remains beneath the Renaissance and Baroque alterations and repairs. The high windows articulate this building of exceptional height and depth, and the quick succession of perpendicular rectangular fields in the main nave and chancel provide the entire structure with a certain rhythm. Around 1300, the presbytery of the new Gothic church of the Knights of St John came into existence, replacing an older Romanesque building.

The proximity of the royal castle brought another important function to the city, namely, it became a place to live; indeed, in subsequent centuries this became one of its most important functions. As early as the fourteenth century, palatial residences of nobles and the high clergy appeared in Malá Strana. The *Palace of the Duke of Saxony and the Archbishop of Mainz* on the southern side of what is now Mostecká street, along with the older Bishop's (later Archbishop's) Court by the area before the bridge, created a kind of residential enclave. Among other buildings of this type were the house of the Bishops of Leitmeritz and some large houses by the little square, Tomášský ryneček, on the site of today's Valdštejnské Square).

Other radical changes occurred in the fourteenth century, especially during the reign of Charles (Karel) IV (1346—1378). These changes affected the two most important structures in the town: the stone bridge and the town walls. The magnificence and creative architectural quality of these two undertakings and other building projects in Malá Strana corresponded to the demanding standards of Charles's era, when Prague was the leader in Gothic architecture.

The Romanesque Judith Bridge was destroyed by the flood of 1342; in subsequent years, a temporary wooden bridge was built upon its ruins. In 1357, there was a ceremonial laying of the foundation stone of the bridge which was later named *Charles Bridge (Karlův most)* after its builder, Charles IV. The architect and supervisor was the designer of the Prague cathedral, Peter Parler. The Old Town bridge tower (Staroměstská mostecká věž) is rightly considered the most beautiful Gothic tower in Europe. The construction of the bridge represented, above all, an excellent achievement of engineering. In contrast to its Romanesque predecessor, the bridge is 5 metres higher, 2.5 metres wider, and instead of the 21 arches of the Judith Bridge, the Charles Bridge is supported by 16 arches with semicircular vaults.

Around 1350, the early Gothic walls of Malá Strana were reinforced, and ten years later Charles IV decided on a radical expansion of the town's territory by building new town walls called the *Hladová zeď (The Hunger Wall)*. Within the southern side of these walls were settlements as far as the street Újezd; they ran up the slope of St Lawrence Hill, which is now called Petřín, continued around the Strahov Monastery and joined the fortification of the village of the serfs of Hradčany, which had been founded on the ridge in the fourteenth century. This project was a part of the grand expansion of the town of Prague as the imperial residence and the seat of the Luxembourg dynasty. The predominant expression of this was the foundation of Nové Město (New Town) which in its time was considered immense. These walls were, of

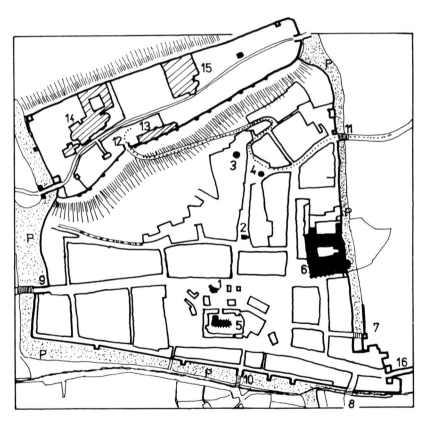

The Gothic town during the last Przemyslides after 1257
(1-Church of St Wenceslas, 2-Church of St Martin below Prague Castle, 3-Church of St Michael below Prague Castle, 4-Church of St Andrew below Prague Castle, 5-Parish church of St Nicholas, 6-Church of St Thomas with the Augustinian Hermits Monastery, 7-Area of the Bishop's Court, 8-Area of the Headquarters of the Knights of St John, 9-Strahov gate, 10-Újezd gate, 11-Písek gate, 12-Southern gate of Prague Castle, 13-Royal Palace, 14-Basilica of St Vitus and adjacent structures, 15-Benedictine Convent with the Church of St George, 16-Judith Bridge)

course, an improvement on the defence of Prague Castle; the first line of defence was thus moved significantly to the south. The perfection of this fortification strategy was proved by the fact that later the seventeenth-century Baroque fortification of Prague's left bank was carried out along its lines.

In 1367, both towns of Prague on the right bank were temporarily incorporated into one whole, named the Greater City of Prague. The town on the west bank below the Castle has since been officially named the Lesser Town of Prague. The name Malá Strana gained popularity, especially at the end of the eighteenth century. With the incorporation of the extensive and still undeveloped area of Petřín into the area within the town walls, medieval Prague acquired its special feature of an immense green tract in the very centre of town.

Malá Strana in the era of Charles IV and his son Wenceslas IV created a very vivid tableau. Besides the great buildings already mentioned, the Archibishop's Palace also acquired a magnificent Gothic appearance in the 1380s, the building of two mighty Gothic churches of the Augustinians and the Knights of St John was completed; they are among the leading pieces of architecture of the period. No less dynamic was the building activity of the burghers. The original regular land division was abandoned and replaced by merging lots for large houses and their later redivision. The former area below the Castle became a lively town with a number of specific functions and a marked degree of autonomy, although its privileges were never as extensive as those of the town on the right bank. The administration of the Lesser Town of Prague was subordinated to the royal chamberlain. On its territory there were also some legally independent parts (with their own by-laws and jurisdiction) administrated by an independent, mainly clerical, authority.

The second half of the fourteenth century was a very complex and dramatic period. In arts and culture, the burgeoning of Gothic was accompanied by humanism. The culmination of social and economic problems found their expression in the sphere of religious thinking. The reformers came out against the worldly power of the Church, and this protest was met with strong support in Prague. Jan Milíč z Kroměříže (d. 1374) preached in the St Nicholas church in Malá Strana, Konrad Waldhauser (c. 1326—1369) was interrogated and held in custody in the Archbishop's Court where the writings of John Wyclif (c. 1330—1384) were publicly burned. When the Hussite revolution began with a burst of violence, on 17 August 1490, churches and monasteries were sacked, including those of the Augustinians and Knights of St John; the lovely Carthusian monastery behind the Újezd gates was completely destroyed. This was only the overture to years of battle for control of Prague Castle, during which all of Malá Strana was destroyed. When, on 7 June 1421, Prague Castle capitulated to the Hussites, the town below it was only an unpopulated field of ruins.

Its reconstruction was carried out very slowly. In 1436, the town had only one third of the houses of the era prior to the Hussite wars. People lived almost exclusively around squares and the main streets, today's Mostecká and Nerudova.

## MALÁ STRANA AT THE END OF THE GOTHIC PERIOD
## AND IN THE RENAISSANCE

The reconstruction of Malá Strana in the mid-fifteenth century was the work of the burghers. The residences of the former authorities remained deserted and later, except for the palace of the Duke of Saxony, disappeared without a trace. The reconstruction of the town was supported by Emperor Zikmund (Sigmund). Not until the rule of Jiří z Poděbrad (George of Poděbrady) (1420—1471) did significant reconstruction of the town begin from the ashes and rubble. In 1460, the king renewed the rights and privileges of the town; four years later the community bought a lot for its town hall in the northeast corner of Malostranské square. In 1478, the northern tower on the Malá Strana side of Charles Bridge was built on the model of Parler's tower on the Old Town (Staré Město) side of the bridge.

The year 1484 was of great importance for the further development and character of Malá Strana. King Vladislav Jagiello made Prague Castle the centre of the kingdom once again. The nobles and tradesmen returned to Malá Strana, but the artists sought employment in the Castle. Although a large fire destroyed 60 houses in the southern and eastern part of Maltézské square, Mostecká street and the area under the jurisdiction of the Knights of Malta (formerly the Knights of St John), Malá Strana prospered to such a degree that the damages were soon repaired. The parish churches were also restored, although they were used primarily by the Utraquists. The monastery buildings, however, were left for years in a makeshift state. The status of monasteries suffered significantly during the Hussite wars. The second half of the fifteenth century and most of the sixteenth century saw the greatest decline in monastic orders; the convents of the Dominicans and Magdalenes were not reconstructed. The chancel of the Church of Our Lady under the Chain was closed, and in 1519 it was vaulted. The Renaissance reconstruction of the Augustinians' Church of St Thomas was carried out in the mid-sixteenth century.

In June 1541, Malá Strana suffered another and more damaging conflagration which destroyed two thirds of the houses of the town; in the history of Malá Strana it was the stylistic dividing line. After the fire, rapid construction took place in the Renaissance style which was incorporated not only into the rebuilding of the destroyed houses but also into many of those that had survived unscathed. The Renaissance style thus significantly changed the look of the town. After the first fire, arcades were built in the buildings on the southern side of Malostranské náměstí; other arcades were then built on the eastern and northern sides of the square and in Tomášská ulice. The new buildings stand out stylistically with their grand gables, arcaded galleries (loggia) and polygonal bay windows on the corners.

In the second half of the sixteenth century, dozens of residences of the nobility appeared in Malá Strana. Only the former palace of the Lords of Hradec *(pánů z Hradce)* situated on the Zámecké schody (Castle Stairs) is preserved in its original state. Zámecké schody was one of two main routes from the town to the Castle; the other led through what is now Nerudova ulice and up the steep slope, where today one finds the Radnické schody (Town-Hall Stairs) to Hradčanské náměstí (Hradčany Square); it then turned towards the western gate of the Castle. Among the other important and well preserved aristocratic residences are the *Hrzánský Palace* on Velkopřevorské náměstí (Grand Prior Square), the *Trčkovský dům* (the Trčka house), which was later incorporated into the western wing of the Valdštejnský Palace, the *Kinský Palace* and the *Šternberk Palace* (which forms the western part of the newer Michnovský Palace).

The story of the *Smiřický Palace* on the north side of Malostranské square testifies to the fact that the architecture of the burghers was, at its best, comparable to the leading projects of the nobles. It was formed by connecting the eastern half of the palace with the western half which had been the house named after its burgher owner Chlupovský. It was bought in 1612 for its palatial dimensions and value.

A very picturesque and well-preserved example of Renaissance burgher architecture is the house called *U Zlatých labutí* (At the Golden Swans) on Pětikostelní square, which was designed before 1590 by the court architect Ulrico Aostalli.

In the Renaissance, the building of houses spread to the area which was once gardens and undeveloped spaces. This is true of the construction of Vlašská and Břetislavova streets; the urban planning is also by Aostalli. The authentic Italian character of these houses is unparalleled in the Renaissance north of the Alps in this period.

The Knights of St John financed the construction of other houses on their land. This is how the Velkopřevorské square came into existence and how construction of the Kampa area began. At the end of the sixteenth and beginning of the seventeenth century there occurred the Renaissance rebuilding of the headquarters of the Knights of Malta (formerly the Knights of St John, who had been renamed by the head of the order at the island of Malta). At the same time, their church was rebuilt. At the beginning of the seventeenth century the Augustinian monastery adjoining the Church of St Thomas underwent extensive reconstruction.

With the imperial court of Rudolph II now in Prague, many foreign artist and artisans were attracted to the city and settled in their own communities. The most tightly-knit group was undoubtedly the Italian community which was situated in the area of Břetislavova, Tržiště (Marketplace), Karmelitská, and Vlašská streets. At the top of Vlašská (which means Italian in old Czech) they built their own hospital and a small church. The German community left its mark with the Lutheran *kostel Nejsvětější Trojice* (Church of the Holy Trinity, 1611—1613) in the block west of Karmelitská street; it is the work of the court architect Giovanni Maria Filippo, who continued in the style of the Roman architecture of that period and thus introduced the principles of early Baroque to Prague.

Around 1600 the political and economic power of the municipality came to a peak. It was manifested in the purchase of the ruins of the

Saxon House and its subsequent rebuilding in a grand Renaissance style to serve the municipality's purposes. The extensive and artistically demanding reconstruction of the town hall was also undertaken prior to 1618, probably based on a plan by Battista Bussi, a Malá Strana builder who had rebuilt the Strahov monastery.

## THE BAROQUE CITY OF MALÁ STRANA

In the same year that the town hall was completed, the Thirty Years War broke out. Its first stage ended two years later with the Battle of the White Mountain (Bílá hora). Prior to the arrival in Prague of the victorious Catholic forces the news went around that the houses of faithful Catholics, which had been marked with a picture of the Virgin Mary, would be spared. These pictures have been preserved, although restored in the Baroque style, on the facades of some Malá Strana houses.

Malá Strana did not escape the subsequent social upheavals and great changes in the ownership of property, which were connected with the great exodus of non-Catholics from the country. Entrepreneurs and speculators were able to acquire massive amounts of property in the course of several years. Without a doubt the toughest and most capable in accumulating personal wealth was the famous leader of the imperial army, General Albrecht von Waldstein (also, Wallenstein or Valdštejn). Through buying and trading he amassed large tracts of land in Malá Strana, on which he started to build a massive complex of palaces in 1623. In the southern part of the *Waldstein Palace* is one of the biggest palace gardens in Prague. What today is Valdštejnské square was built as part of the palace in front of the main facade. The architect of this building, one of the greatest artistic achievements of its period in Prague, was Andrea Spezza (d. 1628). His architectural solution for the complex provides an interesting example from the period between Mannerism and early Baroque on a monumental scale.

The Counter-Reformation with its policy of re-Catholicization returned, of course, great power to the institutions of the Church. Shortly after the Battle of the White Mountain, monasteries and convents were established in Malá Strana. The Dominicans returned to their old monastery on Karmelitská ulice. The nearby Lutheran church, of the Holy Trinity, was reconsecrated Our Lady Victorious and the Carmelites took it over in 1624 and built a monastery nearby. The Carmelite nuns settled in Josefská ulice in 1657. The Theatin Order settled in the Renaissance building adjoining the Zámecké schody (Manor Stairs) in 1670. It was, however, the Jesuits who shaped the look of the city more than anybody else. In 1625 they acquired the Church of St Nicholas as their main institution as well as the majority of buildings along its northern side in the area of Malostranské square. Despite the opposition of municipal government the Jesuits also gradually acquired other buildings but they did not begin reconstruction until 1670.

The construction and reconstruction of churches was already in full swing, which is convincingly shown by the development of architecture in Bohemia in the seventeenth century. Around 1640, *the Church Pan-ny Marie Vítězné* (Our Lady Victorious) was rebuilt; its facade was moved to its eastern side. The new main facade was most probably built based on a plan provided by Rome and is related to the Roman solution for the facade by Giovanni Battista Soria, which had been built to commemorate the victory of the Catholics at the White Mountain. From the 1640s construction of the *Dominicans' monastery* began in Malá Strana; its monumental church, St Mary Magdalene, was designed by Francesco Caratti in 1652. Christoph Dientzenhofer completed the plan in about 1709. This church, with a pair of towers and octagonal cupola in the centre, is one of the most beautiful Baroque churches and is known for its exceptionally richly decorated interior. After the monastery was closed in 1783, it was twice rebuilt in the Classical style. Today it holds the state archives.

In 1670, the Jesuits began the construction of new buildings on the sites of houses they had previously acquired in the area of Malostranské square. The first plan for the rebuilding of the church and the *seminary* was prepared by Caratti in 1671. Only after 1676 did construction begin, based on a new plan by Giovanni Domenico Orsi. After Orsi's death in 1679, construction was taken over by Francesco Lurago and finished in 1687. At that time, however, only the seminary had been built. Even the Romanesque chapel of St Wenceslas had to make way for this new construction. There was, however, no money for the rebuilding of the St Nicholas church. The reconstructed block of the seminary was not a happy undertaking from the point of view of urban planning. Its huge and bulky presence exceeded the dimensions of the square and created a disagreeable impression.

The Carmelite nuns, who in their simple convent set deep into the block of buildings east of Josefská street were cut off from the outside world, decided to build the convent *Church of St Joseph*, in 1686. Its architect, unfortunately, remains anonymous. Its interior is built on an oval floorplan based on the contemporary architecture of Rome and is one of the most remarkable architectural feats of its era. Although two men, Carl Rainaldi and Francesco Borromini in Rome, came up with the original concept, the actual work is unified and creative. The exceptional facade, which is the result of changes in the plan during construction, is inspired by the heavy forms of Flemish Baroque. Its designer was the builder and monk *Ignatius à Jesu* who had previously worked in Louvain.

After settling in Malá Strana, the Theatin order also planned the construction of a new church in what is now Nerudova ulice. The first plan is from 1679 and was provided by the monk Guarino Guarini (1624—1683) of Torino, a leading architect of the High Baroque. His perfectionism and dynamic composition in the undulating facade surpassed both the architectural norms of Prague in those days as well as the abilities of the local builders. The construction of the *Church Panna Marie Božské Prozřetelnosti* (Our Lady of Divine Providence) began in 1691 based on another, Classically inspired plan most probably by the famous French architect Jean Baptiste Mathey (1630—1696) who was active in Bohemia from 1675 to 1695. It was completed under the supervision of Giovanni Santini (1677—1723) only in 1717.

The Jesuits of Malá Strana were not able to accumulate sufficient financial means to be able to begin the construction of the *Church of St Nicholas* (kostel svatého Mikuláše) until the beginning of the eighteenth century. They managed to employ the Malá Strana burgher *Christoph (Kryštof) Dientzenhofer*, the most important architect in Bohemia at the time. The building, as he designed it, is entirely in the radical Baroque style, following basic aesthetic motifs of Guarino Guarini, which were independently developed and raised to a higher level. This is convincingly illustrated by the powerful undulations of the facade as well as the dynamic interior formed along the curved lines of the floorplan and the vaulting which in its construction is very complex. In 1711, the construction had to be stopped due to lack of financial resources; it was not completed until 1737, based on a new plan by Kilian Ignaz Dientzenhofer (1689—1751) who, as opposed to his father, significantly enlarged the eastern part of the church with the presbytery, cupola and belfry. With this solution, K. I. Dientzenhofer was able to suppress the negative influence of the adjacent seminary building on the surrounding buildings. He subordinated the whole space to the new and beautiful architectural dominance of the cupola and belfry. This has become Malá Strana's architectural centre of gravity.

In connection with the work of K. I. Dientzenhofer, one must mention his High Baroque reconstruction of the Gothic-Renaissance Church of St Thomas, from 1721—31. For this church, which is adjacent to the Augustinian monastery, he created a dynamic facade and gave the long interior an expressive rhythm and artistic gradation from the entrance up to the main alter.

Church architecture was undoubtedly at the head of the artistic development of Baroque Malá Strana and Bohemian Baroque in general; the appearance of the town, however, was also formed by the palatial buildings. Prague, as the seat of provincial government and as the social centre, did not lose its attractiveness as a residential area, not even after the imperial court left definitively for Vienna in 1612. While early Baroque palaces were too large and rigid for their surroundings (for example the *Nostitz Palace* on Velkopřevorské square), High Baroque buildings suit their surroundings due to their more sophisticated elements: the gradual exaggeration of scale, the compositional attractiveness of the facade and the creation of a dominant element, a local landmark, in the area. The foremost examples are the buildings by *Giovanni Battista Alliprandi* from 1700 to 1720: the *Kaiserstein, Hartig,* and *Šternberk palaces* on Malostranské square, which are a row of buildings incorporated into a block of houses, and the former *Lichtenstein Palace* on Kampa and the *Lobkowitz (or Lobkovic) Palace* on Vlašská street, which are designed as detached houses of the château type. While the palace on Kampa was changed through its reconstruction in the spirit of historicism in the nineteenth century, the Lobkowitz Palace on Vlašská Street is preserved in its original state and is one of the most beautiful Baroque palaces in Central Europe.

Another important architect of the Czech nobility was *František Maxmilián Kaňka* (1674—1766). His remarkable work in Malá Strana includes the plans for the *Vrtba (Vrtbovský) Palace* in Karmelitská street and *Ledebourg (Ledeburský) Palace* on Valdštejnské square; both are from about 1720. They are especially noteworthy for the rich rhythmical articulation their lower section, the parterre, which is connected with the palace by richly decorated open halls, *sala terrena*, up to the terraces that rise toward the landmark on the highest part of the property. The spaces of the Vrtba Gardens (Vrtbovská zahrada) are decorated with the sculptures of *Matthias Bernhard Braun* (1684-1738), the most important sculptor of the Czech Baroque, who worked together with Kaňka.

*Antonio Lurago* displayed his sense of compositional mastery of material elements in his plans for the reconstruction of the originally Renaissance *Thun (Thunovský) Palace* on Thunovská street below Hradčany. The work of *Johann Georg Aichbauer* is characterized by his ability to graduate subtly the intimate space of the dreamy little square in his solution for the construction of the *Buquoy (Buquoyský) Palace* on Velkopřevorské square (c. 1735). Santini, who worked mainly for the great monasteries outside Prague, left his mark on the architecture of Malá Strana primarily with two beautiful palaces. The front wing of the *Kolowrat Palace* (later known as the Thun-Hohenstein Palace) in Nerudova street, from the years 1716 to 1721, is the strongest echo of Roman building in Baroque Prague. The nearby *Morzin Palace* has a remarkably inventive facade with sculptural ornamentation by F. M. Brokof (1688—1731).

Christoph and Kilian Ignaz Dientzenhofer did not build any palaces in Malá Strana but they had a significant impact on the architecture of the town's houses. Christoph, together with Thomas Haffenecker, created beautiful Baroque houses on the newly surveyed Míšeňská street which at the beginning of the eighteenth century was supposed to bring together businesses and trade that had been disturbing the neighbourhood with their noise; it represents the most striking attempt at urban planning in Baroque Malá Strana. Kilian Ignaz is also the creator of several remarkable houses of which the most beautiful is probably *U dvou hrdliček* (At the Two Doves) in Nosticova street. The facade of the house *U zlatého jelena* (At the Golden Stag) in Tomášská street is also remarkable; its main motif is the monumental sculpture of St Hubert, by F. M. Brokof, which is effectively incorporated into the whole. These outstanding achievements affected the high level of the other, often anonymous, production of dozens of remarkable painted facades which frequently have poetic names and beautifully executed signs.

Charles Bridge at the beginning of the eighteenth century was decorated with monumental sculpture representing patron saints and individual religious orders and monasteries. This remarkable gallery was created by the great sculptors of the Bohemian High Baroque, Matthias Bernhard Braun, Ferdinand Maxmilian Brokof, Johann Brokof (1652—1718), Franz Preiss (c. 1660—1712), and Matthias Wenzel Jäckel (1655—1738). Baroque sculpture, which is able to organize and spiritualize a space, entered the area of Malá Strana. The most remarkable of these sculptures is Brokof's *St John the Baptist* on the northern part of Maltézské square.

The effective motif of the aesthetic harmony of upper Malostranské square is the *plague column* of 1715, which was erected after the ending of one of the worst epidemics of that time. It is based on a design by Alliprandi and was decorated by the sculptors Johann Oldrich Mayer and Ferdinand Geiger. The foot of the Town-Hall Stairs (Radnické schody) was decorated around 1710 with two sculptures; the older, a statue of St John of Nepomuk, is the work of F. M. Brokof; the author of the newer statute, representing St Joseph, remains anonymous.

High and Late Baroque gave Malá Strana its definitive aesthetic expression. Its artists transformed the original Gothic and Renaissance look of the town into a fabulous theatre of purely Baroque imagination and skill. Their solutions are thoroughly in harmony with the broader context of the town. Precisely this ability to transform an older urban whole into a new artistic effect in the Baroque style gives the architecture of Malá Strana an immutable uniqueness. The Baroque art of Malá Strana was unique because it was created by people who actually lived here. Allipardi, Haffenecker, the two Dientzenhofers, Santini, Lurago, and others, were all burghers of Malá Strana.

The high level of Baroque architecture in Malá Strana lasted until the end of the eighteenth century. Some of the significant works of this period are the several Rococo palaces, for example the *Kaunitz Palace* in Mostecká street and the *Turba Palace* on Maltézské square. The splendid epilogue to the Baroque in Malá Strana, which came around 1780, is the *Kolowrat Palace* on Valdštejnská street, especially its almost theatrical and frivolously Rococo terraced garden which was designed by Ignaz Jan Nepomuk Palliardi (1737—1824).

## BETWEEN THE PAST AND FUTURE — THE NINETEENTH AND TWENTIETH CENTURY IN MALÁ STRANA

Around 1770 the most important period in the development of architecture and art in Malá Strana came to an end. The look of the town was now more or less complete. The work that was done from that point on was neither substantial nor especially striking; in several cases it even damaged the town's historical value or overall appearance. The decline in building activity was certainly connected with the gradual lose of the social and economic power of the main builders, the Church and the nobility. In 1773 the Jesuit order disappeared, and the reforms of Joseph II affected many monasteries, including the Dominican (in whose catacomb members of the Dientzenhofer family are buried). Several smaller parish churches were closed down and the building ventures of the nobility declined in number.

In 1791, the facades of the Lichtenstein buildings on upper Malostranské square were merged in the spirit of early Classicism based on a plan by Matthias Hummel. The *Rohan Palace* on Karmelitská street is an important building of late Classicism at its peak. The unique Classical facades of the houses of the burghers are the result of ordinary repairs and reconstruction without any special thought to aesthetics. The court house on Karmelitská has the typical rigid appearance of the bureaucratic buildings of the nineteenth century.

In 1784, the various towns of Prague were incorporated into one single city. Malá Strana became a less important but nevertheless promising part of the greater whole. A change of opinion on housing standards for the wealthier citizens caused part of the population to leave, and in the second half of the nineteenth century Malá Strana became a picturesque and nostalgic but forgotten corner of a nascent metropolis. Life and development were pulsing in other parts of Prague, and Malá Strana's relatively intense cultural life at the end of the eighteenth and beginning of the nineteenth century is but a memory. The construction of the suspension bridge at Újezd, which connected Nové Město (New Town) and the industrial suburb of Smíchov, inspired late Classical construction only on the southern periphery of Malá Strana.

Prior to 1850, the planned railway to Smíchov posed a serious threat to Malá Strana. Thanks to the decisive resistance of the nobleman Vojtěch Lanna, one of the first great Czech entrepreneurs and a connoisseur of history and the arts, the project was never realized.

At the end of the nineteenth century, plans for the reconstruction of Malá Strana in the spirit of contemporary urban planning principles were prepared on more than one occasion. They included the tearing down of a number of historical buildings and the preservation of only the most important buildings as oases in apartment blocks. Thankfully, these plans were only partially realized, for example, the regulation and construction of the street Újezd, the house on the corner of Mostecká street, two apartment blocks in the southern end of Nerudova street, and the northeast block of houses at Klárov. Below the slope of the Letná fields, the monumental building of the former *Strakova akademie* was built, from 1893 to 1895, based on a plan by Václav Roštapil; this is undoubtedly the most important manifestation of historicism in Malá Strana.

The construction of the Mánes Bridge in 1910 created another link between Staré Město and Malá Strana. In the same period, under pressure from the artists and the cultural community, plans for the radical reconstruction of Malá Strana were abandoned. The value of Malá Strana was understood and preserved as one of the great cultural treasures of the past. The priority to conserve historical and artistic monuments remains a determining factor in the use of Malá Strana, an urban complex of world significance.

# WHAT OUGHT TO BE SEEN
# IN MALÁ STRANA

## KRÁLOVSKÁ CESTA

*(King's Road)*. The name itself indicates the main historical commu-
nication line connecting Charles Bridge with the Prague Castle. It is
composed of Mostecká street, Malostranské square, and Nerudova
street. In earlier times (from the fourteenth to the sixteenth centuries),
the main way into the centre of the kingdom was along what is now
called Zámecké schody (the Manor Stairs). The *Charles Bridge (Karlův
most)* has linked both banks of the Vltava since the fourteenth century.
Its construction remains in the original Gothic style (although it has often been repaired). The bridge is decorated with 30 sculptures, originat-
ing mainly from the Baroque period, which form a lovely gallery of
eighteenth-century Czech sculpture. Among the artists who created
these fine pieces were the Brokofs, Braun and Jäckel.

Many of the sculptures have been replaced with copies, and only
eight of the sculptures are, in fact, earlier than the nineteenth and twentieth century.

Of the two towers on the *gate bridge on the Malá Strana side*, the
lower one, on the south side, is Romanesque. It was part of the Judith
Bridge which was destroyed in the flood of 1342. On its eastern facade
is a Romanesque relief which today is concealed inside the adjacent
building, a former customs-house. The northern tower and the connecting gates date from the year 1464.

The *Customs-house (Celnice)*, at Mostecká 1. The little house attached
to the southern tower is from the Renaissance and has a Classical facade
from the nineteenth century. It was formerly the Office of the Prague
Bridge as well as the Prague Salt Office.

*MOSTECKÁ ULICE (Bridge Street)* is clearly an important street of Malá Strana. It was firmly established as early as the twelfth century after
the appearance of the Judith Bridge. In the thirteenth and fourteenth
centuries it was the town's main street; in the time of Charles IV a few
important palaces stood here. The houses are today entirely of Gothic
origin, but after fires and other kinds of destruction, they were rebuilt
in the Renaissance and especially Baroque style, which determines the
atmosphere of the street till today.

*Saský dům (Saxon House)*, Mostecká 3. This mighty Renaissance
building from 1592 stands on the site of a Gothic palace of the Dukes
of Saxony. The facades were repaired in a simple Classical style in 1826.
The house has a fine courtyard with arcades.

*U tří zlatých zvonů (At the Three Golden Bells)*, Mostecká 16. In the
courtyard of this house there is a Gothic tower preserved from the first
half of the fourteenth century. It is a remnant of the former court of the
archbishops of Prague. The Gothic appearance of the residence was destroyed in 1419, and in the seventeenth century this was the site of
a Carmelite monastery.

*Kounický palác (Kounitz Palace)*, Mostecká 15. The original Rococo architecture is the work of Antonín Schmidt (1723—1783). The facade is decorated with the sculpture of Ignaz Franz Platzer (1717—1787).

## MALOSTRANSKÉ NÁMĚSTÍ

*(Lesser Town Square)* was surveyed in 1257 as a large rectangular space that rises westward. The parish church of St Nicholas and other buildings in its space have divided the large square into two smaller squares ever since the Middle Ages: Horní and Dolní Malostranské náměstí (the upper and lower squares); the lower square has three important monuments on its east side:

*Malostranská radnice (Town Hall)*, at Malostranské 21, has been on this spot since 1464. The present building is the result of the merging of two medieval houses that were rebuilt, in 1618, in the Mannerist style, based on a plan by Giovanni Battista Bussi (c. 1550—1622). In 1575, the Bohemian Confessions were written here, which were a collection of demands for religious freedom for non-Catholics in Bohemia and which received the legal recognition of Emperor Rudolph II.

*U Flavínů (At the Flavins)*, Malostranské 22, is a beautiful house of a wealthy burgher family. It was built by Vít Flavín von Rottenfeld on the site of two Gothic houses, one of which had been a printing office since 1502. Today, it is in the Renaissance style with a late Baroque facade.

*Kaisersteinský palác (Kaiserstein Palace)*, Malostranské 23, was built in 1700 from a plan by G. B. Alliprandi. From 1908 to 1914, the world famous diva Ema Destinová lived here. The burghers' houses on the southern side of the lower Malostranské square are of a thoroughly Gothic origin, later rebuilt and connected. Their arcades have been preserved, and their facades were partially repaired in the nineteenth century.

*Petržilovský dům (Petržil House)*, at Malostranské 1, is the biggest house of a burgher family in Malá Strana. It has Gothic cellars that date back to the founding of the town. It reached its present dimensions through Renaissance reconstruction around 1600; at this time the bay-window was built on its corner. The third story was increased in height in 1782, and in the same year the facade was repaired in the Classical style.

*Dům u tří medvědů (The House at the Three Bears)*, at Malostranské 2, is a building which is both of Gothic origin and still has a quite a bit of medieval masonry. From 1436 through the 1480s, the building housed the Malá Strana town hall. The northern side of Malostranské náměstí is formed by three buildings, two of which are the following important residences.

*Palác Smiřických (Smiřický Palace)*, at Malostranské 18, is sometimes also called the Montag Palace. It was built in 1612 by connecting two large Renaissance houses (which had stood on the site of four Gothic houses). The architecture of the interior retained its Renaissance appearance, the walls of the courtyard are decorated with valuable sgraffito. The late Baroque facade dates from 1763 and is based on a plan by the architect Josef Jäger (1772—1793). Prior to the Thirty Years' War, the house belonged to Albrecht Smiřický ze Smiřic. On May 22, 1618, non-Catholic nobles met here in secret and agreed to come out against the emperor. The next day, a conflict with the imperial governors ended with their defenestration from a window of the Prague Castle. This event became the beginning of the uprising of the Prague Estates and the war that would last till 1648.

*Šternberský palác (Šternberk Palace)*, at Malostranské 19, was built on the site of three medieval houses. One of them had caught fire, in 1541, and destroyed two thirds of Malá Strana and Hradčany. The High Baroque appearance that it has today dates from 1720, when it was reconstructed from a plan by Alliprandi. From the mid-eighteenth century through the beginning of the nineteenth century, it was one of the centres of cultural life of Czech society. Its owner at the time, František Josef, Duke of Šternberk, and his relatives, Jáchym and Kašpar Maria ze Šternberka, were important scholars who surrounded themselves with other men of learning. Kašpar Maria was a friend of Laplac, Couvier, von Humboldt and Goethe. In 1770, the house was the site of the founding of the Royal Bohemian Society of Learning, which was the first scientific and scholarly society in Bohemia. In 1796, the house saw the founding of the Society for Patriotic Friends of the Arts, which was the predecessor of the current National Gallery.

The neighbouring house, at Malostranské 20, is in the Renaissance style and dates from sometime after 1580. In close proximity to lower Malostranské square is the *Kostel sv. Tomáše (Church of St Thomas)*, in Letenská street. It is a monumental building, which was originally Gothic and built in the years 1285—1379. It was redesigned in its present Late Baroque style by K. I. Dientzenhofer from 1721—1731. The especially dynamic main facade is very effective; it was ornamented with the even older statue of St Augustine from 1684, made by Hieronymus Kohl (1632—1709). Similarly, the interior was effectively redesigned in the Baroque style and superbly decorated by leading Baroque artists. The vaults are decorated with frescoes from 1728—1730 by Wenzl Laurenz Reiner (1689—1743). In the nave are scenes from the life of St Augustine, in the cupola and presbytery there are scenes from the life of St Thomas the Apostle. The main alter is decorated with smaller, silver-coated statutes by F. Brokof, from 1731, and a larger statue by Johann Anton Quittainer (1709—1765). The alterpieces are copies of originals by Rubens which are now in the National Gallery in Prague. (The originals were acquired for the church in 1637 directly from Rubens's studio in Antwerp). In the chancel in front of the main alter are two small alters consecrated St Sebastian (with a painting by Bartolomäus Spranger) and St Rochus (with a painting by Francis Xavier Palko). The other higher alter in the chancel has paintings of the Assumption of the Virgin Mary, and the Holy Trinity by Karel Škréta, from 1644, and is decorated with sculptures by K. Miller and I. F. Weiss. The main alter and the two larger side alters in the chancel are based on a plan by K. I. Dientzenhofer. Similarly, the triple nave west of the chancel is abundantly furnished with Baroque alters decorated with the work of the leading Czech artists of the Baroque. The eastern part of the northern aisle of the church and the adjacent sacristy have been preserved in their original Gothic state. (The church is open to the public daily from 11.00 am to 12.15 pm and on Sundays from 5.00 pm to 6.00 pm).

*Klášter augustiniánů-poustevníků (Monastery of the Augustinian Hermits)*, in the vicinity of the church of St Thomas, is also of Gothic origin. It attained its present Early Baroque form through reconstruction in the years 1604 to 1634. The chapel of St Barbara in the eastern wing is the original Gothic part of the capitular hall; on its alter is the outstanding painting of the Madonna with St Catherine and St Barbara by J. Heintz from around 1600.

The area of upper and lower Malostranské square is divided by a block of houses including the picturesque group of burghers' homes with Baroque and Classical facades.

The building *U kamenného stolu (At the Stone Table)*, at Malostranské 28, deserves special attention; it acquired its present appearance after the reconstruction of two houses, after 1780, from a plan by Josef Jäger. The building is home to one of the most popular Prague cafes. This block, though, is dominated, by the *kostel svatého Mikuláše (Church of St Nicholas)* whose main facade faces upper Malostranské square. This monumental construction stands on the site of an older Gothic parish church which the Jesuits replaced with the present High Baroque building in two stages, 1703—1711 and 1737—1751. The designer of the first stage (the western part of the church with the main facade) was Christoph Dientzenhofer; the designer of the second stage (the completion of the nave and the building of the cupola, presbytery and belfry) was his son, Kilian Ignaz Dientzenhofer. The main facade is decorated with sculptures by J. B. Kohl-Severa from 1710; on the southern facade is the statute of Faith by Ignaz Franz Platzer from 1760; the apse of the church contains sculptures by Richard and Peter Prachner from around 1770. The exceptionally effective interior is one of the most beautiful examples of Baroque architecture north of the Alps, and its ornamentation dates mainly from the mid-eighteenth century. On the vaults of the nave is a fresco of the Glorification of St Nicholas, by Johann Lukas Kracker; the other frescoes on the cupola, presbytery and choir are the work of Palko. The frescoes in the aisle chapels were created by Joseph Hager, Kracker and J. Kramolín. The sculptural decoration on the interior is mainly the work of Platzer. The pulpit was created by the Malá Strana marble-worker F. Lauermann and is decorated with the sculptural work of Peter Prachner. The alterpieces are mainly the work of important painters of the mid-eighteenth century, Ignaz Raab Palko and Kracker. The set of very early Baroque paintings on the galleries of the church form a cycle representing the Passion; the artist is Škréta, whose Crucifixion is on the alter in the chapel of St Barbara. The magnificent Baroque organ is the work of T. Schwarz, from the years 1745—1746. On his visits to Prague, Mozart played this organ. The interior of the church is exceptionally well preserved and is among the most valuable examples of Baroque interiors. (The church is open for visits from 9.00 am to 5.00 pm).

*The Jesuit Seminary* north of the church was built on the site of a number of older buildings which the Jesuits acquired after 1623. This monumental, rigorous Early Baroque building was built after 1673 from a plan by Orsi. (The small Romanesque church of St Václav used to stand in the area of the northwest corner of the building.)

*HORNÍ MALOSTRANSKÉ NÁMĚSTÍ* (Upper Lesser Town Square). The southern side of this area is formed by a number of valuable burgh- ers' houses which are mostly of medieval origin. In some of the cellars there are remnants of the early Gothic town walls of Malá Strana. To- day, the houses have charming late Baroque and Classical facades. Of special merit is the house *U Palliardiů (At the Palliardi)*, at Malos- transké square 6, which at the end of the eighteenth century belonged to the architect I. Palliardi who rebuilt it after 1778. The house *U zlaté- ho lva (At the Golden Lion)*, which stands at the end of a row of houses with arcades, has a well conserved facade in the Renaissance style circa 1600. The adjacent house *U tří korun (At the Three Crowns)*, rebuilt in the Classical style, was the property of the Miseroni family, famous dia- mond cutters and makers of crystal jewellery.

*Hartigovský palác (Hartig Palace)*, at Malostranské 12, is the last house in this row on the west side of the square. Its precious High Ba- roque architecture appeared around 1700 based on plans by Alliprandi.

The entire western side of the upper square is taken up by the *Licht- ensteinský palác (Lichtenstein Palace)*, at Malostranské 13, which was formed by joining a row of older houses after 1620. Its facade is built in the early Classical style from a plan by the architect M. Hummel on the occasion of Emperor Leopold II being crowned King of Bohemia. The "bloody" governor, Karl von Lichtenstein, who initiated the execu- tion of 27 Czech noblemen in 1621 after the defeat of the uprising of the Czech Estates, lived in this palace until his death in 1627.

The statue of the *Nejsvětější Trojice (Holy Trinity)* in the centre of the square was erected in 1715 as a symbol of thanksgiving for the end of the plague in 1713. The architect was Alliprandi and the sculpture is the work of Mayer and Geiger.

*NERUDOVA ULICE* is the street that leads westward up the hill from the northwest corner of upper Malostranské square. It was esta- blished during the land division of 1257. Halfway down the street, in front of the Theatin Church, there was an early Gothic gate in the town walls until 1711. The street, almost untouched, still retains its historic atmosphere, created above all by the charming Baroque facades of the houses and palaces. The house *U tří králů (At the Three Kings)*, at Neru- dova 8, merits special attention. It is a Renaissance house with a Classi- cal facade and was the property of the wife of the jeweller Misaroni, a friend of the painter Škréta.

The house *U tří housliček (At the Three Violins)*, at Nerudova 12, has a sign on its graceful Baroque facade that recalls its owner, the famous violin-maker T. Edlinger.

*Valkounský dům (Valkoun House)*, Nerudova 14, belonged to the fa- mous architect Santini from 1705 to 1723, who rebuilt it. After Santi- ni's death, the goldsmith F. Diesbach bought it and added late Baroque ornamentation to its facade in 1740. In 1760, an outstanding gold-smith, J. Pakeni, bought the house.

*U zlaté číše (At the Golden Goblet)*, Nerudova 16, bears a sign on its graceful Renaissance facade, which recalls its one-time owner, the goldsmith B. Schumann. At the beginning of the eighteenth century it belonged to the artist in stucco, J. Spinetti.

*Thun-Hohensteinský palác (Thun-Hohenstein Palace)*, formerly the Kolowrat Palace, is located at Nerudova 12. This is a superb piece of High Baroque architecture, from 1716-1720, from a plan by J. B. Santini. The sculptural decoration was added by Braun. Today, it is the Italian Embassy. The adjacent *Church Panny Marie Božské Prozřetelnosti (Our Lady of Divine Providence)* was built for the Theatin order in the years 1691 to 1717. The original plan was probably Mathey's; construction was completed by Santini. Its well preserved original interior is decorated with statutes by Mayer and Jäckel. (The church is open to the public Tuesdays and Thursdays from 5.30 pm before mass).

*Morzinský palác (Morzin Palace)*, at Nerudova 5, was built in the seventeenth century by joining four Renaissance houses; its High Baroque facade was made in 1713—14 by Santini. Its rich sculptural ornamentation is the work of F. M. Brokof. The well known atlantes of the two Moors supporting the portal are inspired by figures on the Morzin coat-of-arms. Above the portal there are allegories of Night and Day. On the gable at the top of the facade is an allegory of the "four" continents. The Rumanian Embassy is located here.

*Osel u kolébky (The Ass at the Cradle)*, Nerudova 25, is notable for its Baroque facade from 1706 when it belonged to the artisan cabinet maker J. Nonnenmacher.

*Brettfeldský palác (Brettfeld Palace)*, Nerudova 33, is a Late Baroque building from 1765, by the architect Johann Joseph Wirch. Its builder was J. von Brettfeld, a patron and collector; he hosted Casanova as well as Mozart here.

*U bílé řepy (At the White Beet)*, Nerudova 39, was the property of the Quittainer family in the seventeenth and eighteenth century. Its Baroque facade is decorated with Classical designs.

*U hlubokého sklepa (At the Deep Cellar)*, Nerudova 40, belonged to the sculptor J. O. Mayer.

*U dvou slunců (At the Two Suns)*, Nerudova 47, is valuable because of its early Baroque facade from 1763. In the mid-nineteenth century, the Czech writer Jan Neruda, whose stories about life in Malá Strana are famous, lived here and the street is named after him.

*U tří králů (At the Three Kings)*, Nerudova 2. This predominantly Baroque building was designed as a visual landmark of the upper part of the street.

*Radnické schody (Town-Hall Stairs)*. This route connects Malá Strana with Hradčany. (The street Ke Hradu, which runs up the slope towards the Castle in the direction opposite the stairs was not built until 1644, and is based on a plan by Mathey). F. M. Brokof created the sculpture of St John of Nepomuk at the foot of the stairs in 1710. The other sculpture of St Joseph dates from 1714; its artist is unknown.

Other important sights which should not be missed:


*Valdštejnský palác (Waldstein Palace)* Valdštejnské square 4, is a monumental Early Baroque and Mannerist building from the years 1623 to 1631. The architect, A. Spezza, designed it for the leader of the imperial army, General Albrecht von Waldstein. The square in front of its facade was built at the same time as the palace, after the demolition of a block of houses. The palace spreads out over five courtyards. Its interior is by outstanding Italian artists. East of the palace is a large garden, which has been kept in its original form. The sculptures in the *garden* are the work of Adriaen de Vries, the student of Giovanni da Bologna (1529—1608). (It is open to the public from May to September, every day from 10.00 am to 6.00 pm. The riding halls of the Valdštejnský palác on Klárov street today houses one of the branches of the National Gallery).

[ 27 ]

*Kostel sv. Josefa (Church of St Joseph)*, on Josefská street, is an outstanding building which dates from 1686—1692 and is based on a plan sent by Rome. The facade is from a design by Father Ignatius à Jesu, a Carmelite from Louvain. The decorations of the interior create a remarkable harmony. On the main alter and the alter of St Theresa are outstanding paintings by P. Brandl. The sculptural decoration is the work of Jäckel, pre 1700 and circa 1730. (Open to the public daily, from 10.00 am to 5.00 pm)

*Klášter karmelitek (Convent of the Carmelite nuns)*, on Josefská street, is an Early Baroque building from 1657 to 1672. Nearby is another large garden, *Vojanovy sady (Vojan Park)*, accessible from the street U lužického semináře (At the Lusatian Seminary), which is open year-round, from 8.00 am to 7.00 pm)

*Kostel Panny Marie Vítězné (The Church of Our Lady Victorious)*, on Karmelitská street, is an outstanding early Baroque building which dates from 1611—1613 and is based on a plan by G. M. Filippi. It underwent significant reconstruction around 1640 and acquired the facade that exists today. It became the monastery church of the Carmelite order in 1624. At the main alter is a copy of "the miraculous Marian painting" which is given credit for the victory of the Catholic armies at White Mountain in 1620. The alter itself is High Baroque from 1716. At the alter of the central aisle on the northern side of the nave is a little sculpture of the *Christ Child of Prague*, which is one of the most worshipped images of the Christ Child in the whole Catholic world. This little sculpture was part of the private property of St Theresa of Jesus and by means of the Manriquez family became part of the property of the Czech Pernštejn family. Polyxena von Lobkowitz, née Pernštejn, donated it to the Church of our Lady Victorious in 1628. The alter of the Christ Child of Prague is a splendid Late Baroque work of the marble-worker Lauermann and the sculptor P. Prachner, from 1776. The other alters are early Baroque, three of them (St Joseph's, St Joachim's and St Anne's, and St Šimon of Štok) are decorated with valuable paintings by

P. Brandl from 1715—1716. (The church is open to the public daily from 10.00 am to 5.00 pm).

*Kostel Panny Marie Pod Řetězem (Church of Our Lady under the Chain)* and the *generalát (headquarters) of the Knights of Malta.* This complex is located on Lázeňská street, Maltézské square, and Velkopřevorské square. The headquarters of the order of St John of Jerusalem, known as the Knights of St John (from the sixteenth century, the Knights of Malta), has its origins in 1158. The original Romanesque buildings, however, have disappeared after several reconstructions. The church today is a Gothic building from the fourteenth century, whose presbytery was rebuilt in the Renaissance style in 1610; the triple nave with a pair of towers was never completed. The church's interior was decorated, in 1640, with the help of Carlo Lurago. It contains some outstanding Baroque pieces. At the main alter there is Škréta's painting, "the Miracle of Our Lady in the Battle of Lepant" from 1650. The sculptures are the work of Johann Georg Bendl from 1651. Another of Škréta's paintings is at the alter of St Barbara. The space has precious early Baroque stucco work and Renaissance chancel screens. North of the church is a Baroque *convent* building by Haffenecker from 1728—1730. To the south is the *Grand Prior's Palace,* which is a Renaissance building with significant remmants of medieval structures; it was rebuilt in the Baroque style around 1730. (The church is open to the public on Saturday beginning 5.30 pm, prior to the mass, and on Sunday beginning 9.30 am, prior to the mass).

## Other Important Sights and Romantic Nooks of Malá Strana

*PALACES BELOW THE CASTLE.* Between Klárov and Valdštejnské square is *Valdštejnská ulice (Valdštejnská street)* at the foot of Prague Castle. In the Middle Ages this street connected the core of Malá Strana with a village called Rybáře (also known as svatý Petr and Na písku) near the ford over the Vltava River. Today, it is surrounded by palatial residences, while the whole southern side of the street is taken up by the Waldstein Palace. On the northern side of the street are other remarkable Baroque palaces, some of which date from the Ranaissance and earlier. From Klárov there is the *Fürstenberg Palace* (Valdštejnská 8) from 1743—1747, the *Kolowrat Palace* (Valdštejnská 10), which acquired its present appearance after 1784 from a plan by Palliardi, and the *Palffy Palace* (Valdštejnská 14), which acquired its present appearance around 1712. After a row of Renaissance burgher houses comes the *Ledebourg (Ledeburský) Palace* (Valdštejnská 3); it is located where two Renaissance houses once stood, and its present appearance is the result of reconstruction carried out in 1787 from a plan by Palliardi. Behind the Kolowrat, Palffy and Ledebourg palaces are extraordinarily beautiful *Baroque gardens* which are richly articulated. (They are undergoing long-term reconstruction). West of Valdštejnské náměstí is the triangular *Pětikostelní náměstí (Five Churches Square).* Here, immediately below the Castle, was the very core of the early medieval settlement of Malá Strana before the construction of the Gothic town. Picturesque and lined by valuable Renaissance and Baroque houses, the dead-end street *U zlaté studny (At the Golden Well)*, leading north out of the square, was, until the fourteenth century, the main access route to the former southern gate of the Prague Castle. On the corner of the square and the little street, one's attention is captured by the Renaissance building of *U zlaté labutě (At the Golden Swan)* on Pětikostelní 10, which was constructed after 1589 by the builder Aostalli and preserved in its original state. The western side of the square is dominated by the large early Baroque *Bylandt-Rheidt Palace*, on Pětikostelní 13, from around 1700. Behind it is an early Baroque garden. Further up the slope is the *Thun Palace*, on Thunovská street 14, which is today the British Embassy. The Baroque of the Renaissance building is the result of reconstruction from 1716—1727, from a plan by A. Lurago. This is where Mozart stayed during his first visit to Prague in 1787.

*ZÁMECKÉ SCHODY (Manor Stairs)* was the main route connecting Malostranské square and Prague Castle from the mid-fourteenth to the mid-seventeenth century. The stairs were built in 1672—1674. The space is lined by historical houses of medieval origin with valuable Renaissance, Baroque and Classical facades. The most striking is the monumental *Slavata Palace*, on Zámecké schody 25, which is a stunning sixteenth century Renaissance building. (Today, it is a part of the Italian Embassy).

*U brabantského krále (At the Brabant King)*, Zámecké schody 15, *U zlatého anděla (At the Golden Angel)* on Zámecké schody 23, and *U zlaté růže (At the Golden Rose)* are priceless Renaissance houses; the latter two belonged to the court painter of Rudolph II, Bartolomäus Spranger, in the years 1582 to 1611.

*KAMPA* is a little island between the main stream of the Vltava River and its arm called Čertovka (the Devil's Brook) which also served as a millrace for many mills. Kampa was originally part of Prague's Staré Město, but today it is part of Malá Strana. At Čertovka, north of the Carles Bridge, there is a grouping of historical burgher houses called *Pražské Benátky (the Venice of Prague)*; south of the Charles Bridge is a little square on Kampa, which first appeared in the sixteenth century. Since 1599, pottery markets have regularly taken place here. Of the historical houses, the most striking is the house *U bílé boty (At the White Shoe)*, at Kampa 13, with a rich Rococo facade by Jäger from 1766. *U modré lišky (At the Blue Vixen)*, at Kampa 1, represents delightful Baroque architecture from 1696. South of the square, on the bank of the Vltava, is the *Lichtenstein Palace*, at Kampa 4, which was originally a High Baroque building that was constructed in the years 1696 to 1700 from a plan by Alliprandi. The building was rebuilt in the Renaissance style and made higher in 1864. A *Classical single-family dwelling* stands opposite the palace, at Kampa 7, built by reconstructing a Renaissance tannery in 1797. Count Bedřich Nostitz had it rebuilt. In 1811 the leading Bohemian philologist Josef Dobrovský lived here as a host of the count's family. His monument, erected in 1947, stands just east of the house; the bust was made in 1891 by T. Seidan.

In the twentieth century, the poet Vladimír Holan and the actor and writer Jan Werich lived here. Most of the island is a *park* which was created by joining the three big gardens belonging to noblemen. On the southern side of Kampa, there is the former village of Újezd, which became part of Malá Strana in the fourteenth century. The valuable *Church sv. Jana Křtitele Na prádle (St John the Baptist at the Wash-Place)*. Ist Romanesque predecessor was probably founded in 1142; before 1300, a Gothic church was built in its place and underwent only minor Baroque reconstruction in the eighteenth century. *The statue of St John of Nepomuk* in front of the church is the work of F. M. Brokof from 1715, but was not placed here until 1938. West of the church is a picturesque building of the early Baroque — the Malá Strana *hospital*, on Říční street 6, which was built in 1662 by G. de Capali.

*VELKOPŘEVORSKÉ NÁMĚSTÍ (Gran Prior's Square)*. This charming square south of the Church of Our Lady under the Chain is surrounded mainly by palatial buildings. On the north side are the headquarters of the Knights of Malta; to the east, at Čertovka, is a Renaissance building of the former *Gran Prior's Mill*, on Velkopřevorské 6, whose exterior is preserved in its original state from 1597—1598. The *Palace of the Metychs from Čečov*, Velkopřevorské 1, is opposite the mill and is a valuable Renaissance building from around 1600, with a beautiful Mannerist portal. Beside it, there is the *Large Buquoy Palace*, Velkopřevorské 2, whose late Baroque architecture is by Aichbauer from 1736—1739. The adjacent *Little Buquoy Palace*, Velkopřevorské 3, is a Renaissance building from about 1600 whose facade was modified circa 1780. Both the palaces belong to the French Embassy.

*MALTÉZSKÉ NÁMĚSTÍ AND THE SURROUNDING AREA*. The triangular space of Maltézské náměstí (Maltese Square), located to the west of the Church of Our Lady under the Chain, was formed by the crossroads that were here in the early Middle Ages. All that remains of the routes is the line of *Prokopská street*, where the building *U sv. Prokopa (At St Procopius)*, Prokopská 3, is located. This is a former Baroque church rebuilt in the Classical style on the site of a Romanesque church that dated from about 1200. The neighbouring house, called *Regent*, Karmelitská 20, was originally a Romanesque courtyard and subsequently rebuilt many times. The most impressive of the remaining historical houses are *Sachsenbeck House*, on Prokopská 6, and *U černého koníčka (At the Little Black Horse)*, Prokopská 10, which have valuable Baroque facades. The northern part of Maltézské square is dominated by the sculpture of St John the Baptist, which is the outstanding Baroque work of F. M. Brokof, from 1715. The housing of the square has preserved its historical character and charming facades. *Turba Palace*, on Maltézské 6, which today is the Japanese Embassy, is Rococo architecture by Jäger from 1765—1767. Across the street is the *Palace of the Strakas from Nedabylice*, on Maltézské 14, which is the result of Baroque reconstruction circa 1700; the interior is decorated with valuable frescoes by J. R. Bys of the same period. The southern part of the square is dominated by the gigantic *Nostitz Palace*, on Maltézské 1, today the Embassy of the Netherlands. The Early Baroque building was built by the architect F. Caratti from 1658 to 1660. The facades were modified circa 1767 and 1780. The palace contains the beautiful well-preserved rooms of the Nostitz library, which was one of Prague's best. East of the palace, is the narrow lane, *Nostická street*, in whose southern part one can find a remarkable group of burghers' houses. One of them, *U dvou hrdliček (At the Two Doves)*, Nostická 7, was built by K. I. Dientzenhofer for a friend, the carpenter J. Leffler.

*THE FORMER ITALIAN QUARTER ON MALÁ STRANA.* The area populated mainly by Italians in the sixteenth century is located near the little square *Tržiště* (Market Place) and *Vlašská* street. Until the fourteenth century this territory was outside the walls of Malá Strana and later it was gradually developed. Here, at the foot of Petřín Hill, there were many gardens. The most important building on Tržiště is the monumental Baroque *Schönborn Palace*, Tržiště 15, which today houses the Embassy of the United States of America. It was built in the seventeenth century by joining together six houses and was rebuilt in the High Baroque style from 1715 to 1718, probably by Alliprandi. There is a vast garden behind the palace.

The blocks of houses around Vlašská and *Břetislavova* streets were built at the end of the sixteenth century. Some of them preserved their original Renaissance state and at present are undergoing extensive renovation. Two hundred metres up the road, Vlašská street widens into a charming little square which was built from 1704 to 1707 during the construction of the *Lobkowitz Palace*, on Vlašská 19, which today is the German Embassy. The architect of this building, one of the most beautiful high Baroque palaces in Central Europe, was Alliprandi; minor changes were carried out by Palliardi from 1767 to 1769.

On the other side of the street is a group of valuable houses of which *U zlaté růže (At Golden Rose)*, Vlašská 28, and *U velkého střevíce* (At the Big Slipper), Vlašská 30, are conserved in their original Renaissance state. *Vlašský špitál*, west of the square, was built in the seventeenth century and served as a hospital and poorhouse for the Italian community in Prague; today, it is the home of the Italian cultural centre. The Mannerist hospital *chapel of St Charles Boromeus* is used as a concert hall. The picturesque little streets that are adjacent, *Šporkova, Jánská, and Jánský vršek* — whose historical houses are no less picturesque — are very old and maintain the lines of the routes that led through the medieval village called Obora that had once been here.

*1/   Panorama of Malá Strana from the Old Town embankment*

4/ *Roofs in southern Malá Strana, view from the bridge towers at Malá Strana (In the foreground is Church of Our Lady under the Chain, in the background is the Church Our Lady Victorious*

5/   *Mostecká street, the view from the bridge towers at Malá Strana
(the Church of St Nicholas the landmark, in the background is the
panorama of the Strahov monastery)*

◁ 6/ *The Church of Our Lady under the Chain in Lázeňská street, the two Gothic towers of the front facade (from the mid-fourteenth century)*

7/ *The Church of Our Lady under the Chain, the interior was reconstructed in Renaissance and Early Baroque style in the seventeenth century*

8/  *Sternegg Palace in Lázeňská street, the hall with Baroque
decoration (stucco ceiling, circa 1740, the wall painting is by
L. Seidl, 1774).*

9/ *Maltézské square, full view facing north*

11/ *Nostitz Palace on Maltézské square, the main portal (Palace is Early Baroque, circa 1660, probably by F. Caratti, the main portal is by A. Haffenecker, after 1765)*   ▷

10/ *Turba Palace on Maltézské square (J. Jäger, pre 1767)*

12/ The house at St Florian in Nostická street
    (K. I. Dientzenhofer, 1727)

13/ The house U dvou hrdliček, in Nostická street
    (K. I. Dientzenhofer, 1727)

*15/ Fürstenberg Palace in Valdštejnská street (Baroque, pre 1740)*

16/ *Axial staircase, terraced gardens of the Kolowrat Palace*
*(J. I. N. Palliardi, c. 1770)*

*17/ Waldstein Palace, main facade on Valdštejnské square*
*(A. Spezza, 1623—1630)*

18/ Waldstein Palace, main hall
(A. Spezza, B. Bianco, and Italian stuccoers, c. 1630)

19/   *Waldstein Palace, sala terrena, view from the garden*
      *(G. Pieronni, after 1623)*

20/ *Eastern part of the Waldstein Gardens with Hradčany in the background*

22/ *The house U zlaté labutě at Pětikostelní square (U. Aostalli, c. 1590)*

*24/    Thunovská street*

25/ The house U zlatého jelena in Tomášská street, the portal and sculpture of St Hubert (architecture by K. I. Dientzenhofer, 1723—25, sculpture by F. M. Brokof, 1725)

26/ The statuette of the Christ Child of Prague, in the Church of Our Lady Victorious (This Spanish Mannerist sculpture was donated to the church in 1628 by Polyxena von Lobkowitz)

28/ *Church of St Thomas on Letenská street, interior (Gothic and*
*Renaissance structure rebuilt in the Baroque by*
*K. I. Dientzenhofer, 1727—31, Baroque fresco by V. V. Reiner,*
*Late Baroque interior from time of reconstruction)*  ▷

27/ *Northeast corner of upper Malostranské square (on the right-hand*
*corner is the Lesser Town Town Hall with the Church of St*
*Thomas in the background)*

30/  *Church of St Joseph, cupola of the nave (perhaps by a Roman*
     *architect, designed pre 1687, built 1687—92)*

31/ *Cupola and belfry of the Church of St Nicholas on Malostranské square, view from the east (K. I. Dientzenhofer, 1737—51, with the house U kamenného stolu in the foreground)*

32/ *Church of St Nicholas, main facade*
*(Christoph Dientzenhofer, 1703—11)*

34/ Church of St Nicholas, view of the cupola (K. I. Dientzenhofer, ▷
1737—51, fresco by F. X. Palko, 1753—54)

33/ Church of St Nicholas, main nave (Christof Dientzenhofer,
1703—11, K. I. Dientzenhofer, 1737—51, decoration after 1750)

36/  *Smiřický Palace on Malostranské square (Renaissance structure, late 16th to early 17th century; Late Baroque reconstruction, mid-18th century)*

39/ *Morzin Palace on Nerudova street, with Moors as atlantes (F. M. Brokof, 1714)*

42/   *Statue of St John of Nepomuk at the Town-Hall Stairs*
      *(F. M. Brokof, c. 1710)*

44/   *Malá Strana from the upper pavilion of the Kolowrat Gardens*

*45/ Malá Strana from the southern gardens of Prague Castle*

# A MAP OF MALÁ STRANA